ACCESSING... HISTORY
BRITAIN 1066–1485

CONTENTS

INTRODUCTION

The period from the end of the Saxon era to the victory of the Tudor dynasty at the Battle of Bosworth in 1485 saw remarkable changes as well as long periods where very little changed. In this book the images are principally taken from contemporary handwritten and drawn (or painted) manuscripts, and they reflect the influence of wealthy patrons either within the Church or powerful families. They also reflect the importance of Latin and French as official, religious and administrative languages.

Ordinary working people and peasants are seen within these images, but it would have been very rare for them to have been the ones who would have actually seen and enjoyed them once the manuscripts or books were finished. So these images also reflect the very clear hierarchy of medieval society – a structure based on wealth and power.

Images have been chosen to illustrate the following ten themes:

1. THE FARMING YEAR: what was life like for the medieval peasant?
2. LIFE EVERLASTING: the importance of the Church on medieval life
3. THE WIDER WORLD: images related to trade, exploration and travel
4. THE HUNDRED YEARS WAR: how land and sea battles have been depicted
5. HEALTH AND HYGIENE: how would medieval people cope with minor (or major) illness?
6. THE RISE AND FALL OF CASTLES: a look at the castle as a strategic and status symbol
7. A COMMUNITY APART: how Jews were treated in England and Europe
8. THE JIHAD: how the Crusades were recorded
9. WEALTH AND POVERTY: the contrasting lives of the rich and poor
10. WAS THE MAYOR A MURDERER?: a focus on the Peasants' Revolt

All the images are supported in separate packs by activity ideas and lesson notes at three different levels: Mainstream, SEN and G&T.

Throughout your work with images you may wish to encourage pupils to dig deeply into the composition of images and look beyond pure description, although accuracy of observation and language may be vital and, for that reason, reinforcing some key terms may be helpful. For example:

	Background	
Left	Centre	Right
	Foreground	

as well as atmosphere, colour, composition, context, genre, influences, light, narrative, perspective, purpose, symbolism, technique and tone.

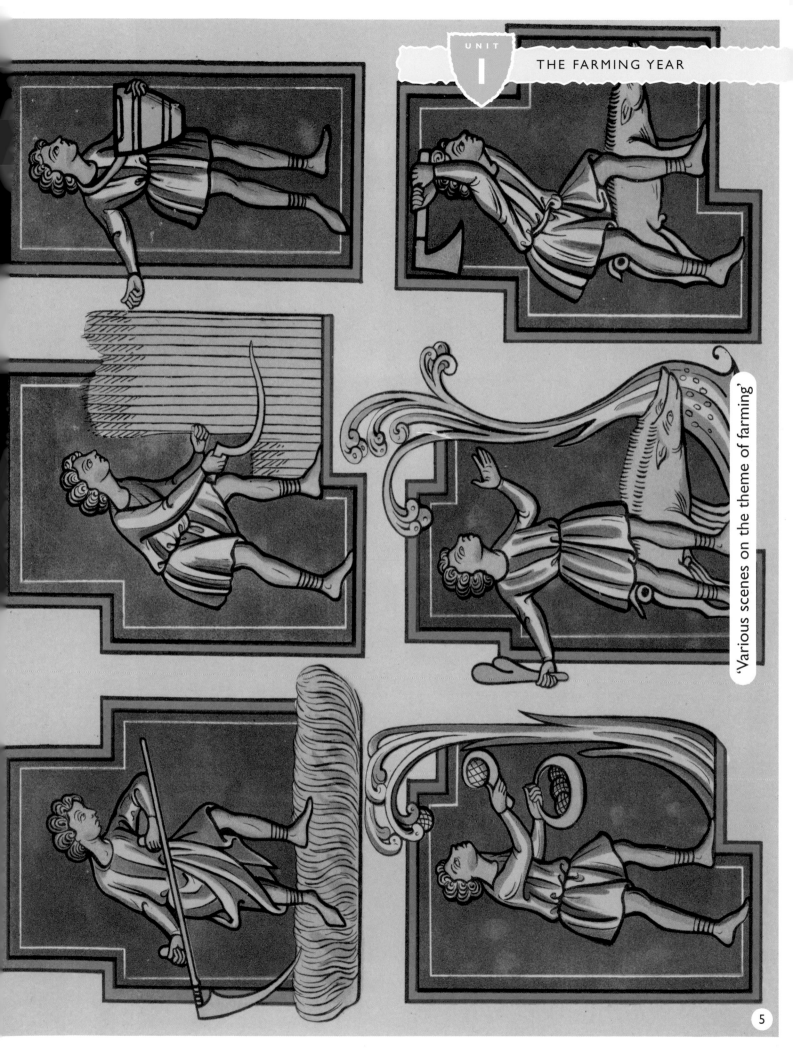

'Various scenes on the theme of farming'

'A peasant family churns butter outside their home'

'Shearing sheep', a miniature calendar page for June

aunt cayin de ceul: estoit mauoist. Dek losnz depleus si senfuit. E
errat tere: 7 semoist ble. E sileuk guidoit estre muce. ke deuk de ceel ne
t pis fuu E ke me out poer ne uertu. E deluy eurt un grauut pais. E
ides genz 7 tutes maudis. La sustenaunce q creuth sur tere Nusl de
ne la uouslt crere. ke deeuk co out este cue de drept dupt aestre borstble
tes estoreiut de male cresunce. Por ceo aufsn lur uiut meschaunce. E a ca
n nureinent. Apres uerrez la grse coment keke sest de deuk madist
eschaunc ara saunz respirt. Enker sura de erttage cayin 7 tut: son hnage
rtuz ceul q ticlon fuit. Touz ensemble en enfer uout.

'Cain and his family ploughing'

A young man with a basket sows seed

Peasants reaping the harvest, being supervised by an official

'Peasants working the land'

9

'The crucifixion'

'The marriage of Phillippa of Lancaster'

A burial scene

sepultura no massa noble
por fer cascun cor lo cors e
la carn morta por cascun
honrar legudament plest

mentque hom enten que
auia cosa glificar enlaltre
segle Estoria deles vij· obres
de o Disericordia ·:~ ! ~ · : ✝

lo bon hom cast ⸱⸱ lo bon hom castiga foyll ⸱:—

lo bon hom dona ⸱ lo bon hom dona amējar e aboure als pobres

lo bon hom alber ⸱⸱ lo bon hom alberga los pobres

lo bon hom uest los ⸱⸱ lo bon hom uest los nus pobres ⸱:—

lo bon hom ufica con ⸱ lo bon hom ufica con forta los malales ⸱:—

lo bo hom ufica ⸱ lo bo hom ufica los encarcerats

lo hom seboler ⸱⸱ lo hom seboler los morts ⸱:—

lo quarto del bo ga ⸱ lo quarto del bo ga tres les obres d media

'The works of mercy'

'Actions of devils'

A world map, 1342

'The Tartar Khan feasting'

'Pepper harvest'

17

'White elephants are presented to Alexander the Great'

Quant le roy dan
gleterre 2 ses ma
reschaulx eurent
ordonnees leurs
bataillesz et leurs naures
moult richement 2 saigemt
Ilz furent tendre et traire
les voiles contremot et vin
drent au vent de quartier
sur dextre po ail lanataige
du souleil qui en venant
leur estoit ou visaige. Si
sauiserent que ce ler puoit
trop muyre et detureret vng

vu et tournoyxent tant qlz
leuent aleur voulente. Les
normans qui les voyxent
tourner, se merueilloient
poz quoy ilz le faisoient 2
disoient, ilz resoignet et
reculent. Car ilz ne sont
pas gens pour combatre a
nous. bn voient les noz
mans sur les baineres q le
roy dangleterre y estoit per
sonnelement. Si myrent
leurs vaisseaulx en bo estat
Car Ilz estoient saiges en

'Battle of Sluys (French for l'Ecluse), 24 June 1340'

19

Two pictures showing the Battle of Crécy, 26 August 1346

'Battle of Poitiers, 1356'

'Battle of Agincourt, 25 October 1415'

'A physician bleeding a patient'

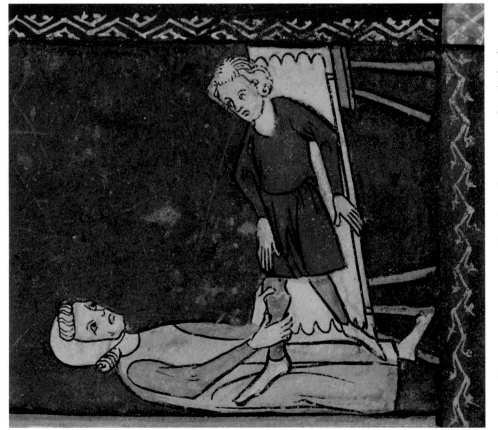

'A woman setting a broken bone in a boy's leg'

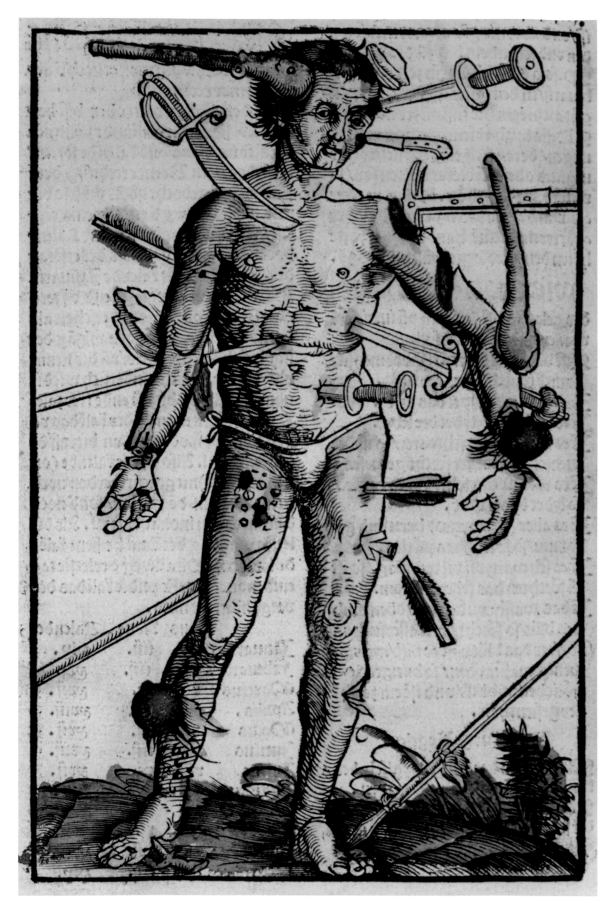

'Wound man'

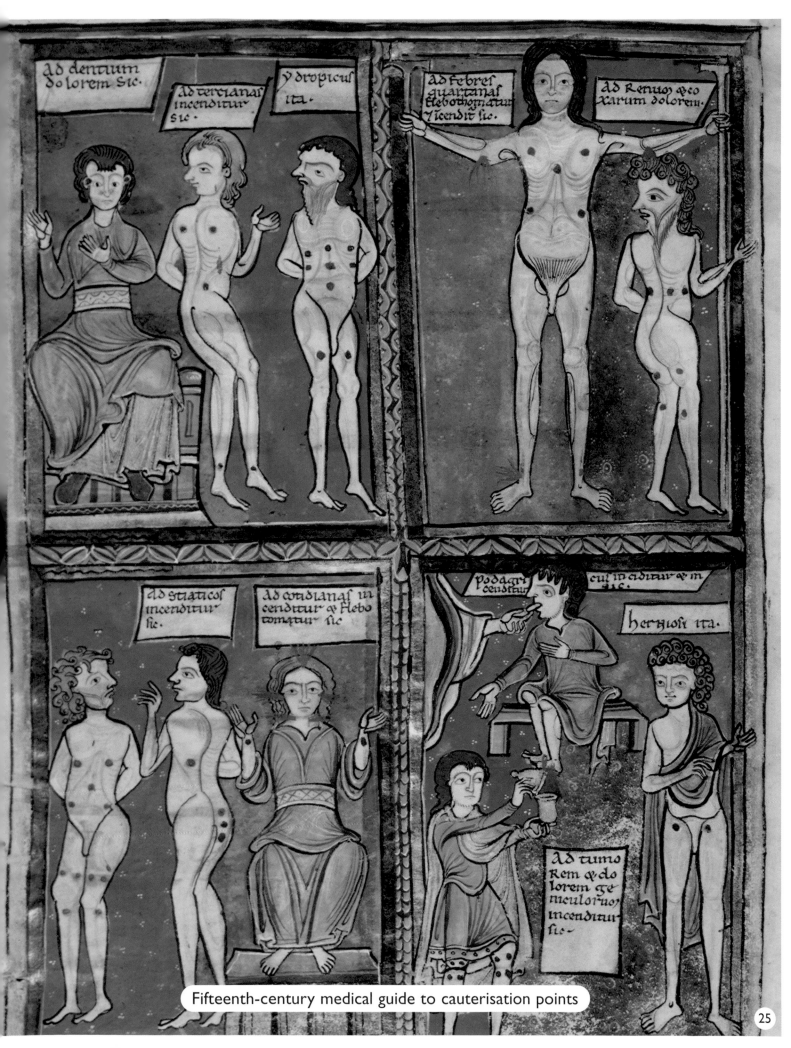

Fifteenth-century medical guide to cauterisation points

25

Fifteenth-century medical guide

*A Verger's Dream: Saints Cosmas and Damian Performing
a Miraculous Cure by Transplantation of a Leg*

The Miracle of the Deacon Justinian

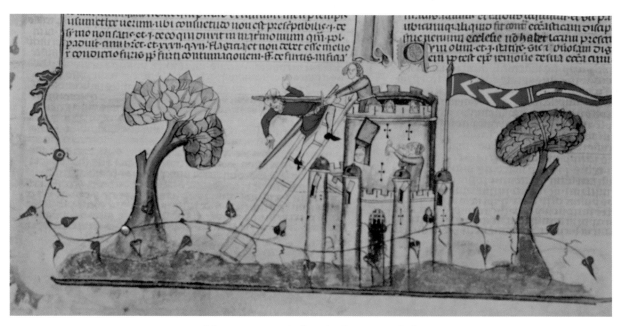

'A woman defends her castle'

'The French destroy Genoa'

Charles, Duke of Orleans, writes while imprisoned in the Tower of London

Arundel Castle, West Sussex

Siege of a fortified town

'Siege of a castle, using a cannon and mortar'

'Persecution of the Jews'

'The Third Crusade of Pastoreaux – Jews throwing
their children from a tower'

'The inside of a synagogue'

'The ritual slaughter and skinning of a sheep for the Passover meal'

Anti-Semitic cartoon, detail from the edge of a Jewish receipt roll

...inton beatus tridentin⁹ puerul⁹. quē ob miraculoꝛ frequētiā bᵗⁱⁿ appellāt. die marꝷ .xij .kaꝯ. apriliſ
...to supꝛa millesimū q̄ter cētū in bebdomoda sctā a iudeiſ
...tem ea in vꝛbe degetes pasca suo moꝛe celebꝛaturi .cuꝛ
...anū nō baberet immolādū cuⁱ⁹ sanguinē in azimis suis vti possent puerū in būc modū in samuelis cu
iusdā iudeī domū furtim depoꝛtarūt. In sacra bebdomoda āñ die pasce luce tercia vespere facto is āñ foꝛeſ
pᷓis pueruli moꝛe sedēs. cū nō aderat genitoꝛ nec cara parēs ꝓditoꝛ tbobias astitit blanda voce moꝛatus
puer cuⁱ⁹ etas nō dū ter dece mēses viderat. fert illico samuel ad edes. Cūqꝫ nox ruit bic gemini saligmā
samuelqꝫ tbobias vitalis moyses ysrabel atꝫ mayer āñ synagogā leti eⁱ⁹ pectoꝛa nudāt. In eius collo pꝛi
mū ne vagire posset sudariolū apposuerūt ꝫ extensis bꝛachijs ꝓmo papulū foꝛpicibꝰ. mox genā dexterā ꝑ
cidentes. Inde q̄sqꝫ foꝛpice carnē ꝗuellit. Sudibꝰ deinde pacut̄ pupugere. cū ille manus alter plantas co
tinet crudeliteꝛ sanguine collecto bymonos eoꝛ moꝛe canētes. addūt minisꝳba. accipias suspese ibesu. fe
cere sic olim maioꝛes nr̄i. sic ꝑfundanꝷ celo terra mariqꝫ xꝑicole. sic caput eius inter vlnas cecidit ꝫ vita li
bera ad superos fecit iter. inde ad cenas ꝑperarūt azimas de sanguine eius in xꝑi dedecⁱ ederūt. eoqꝫ moꝛ
tuo statim coꝛpus in ꝓpinquū domus eoꝛ flumen ꝑiecerūt ꝫ pasca cū gaudio celebꝛarūt. Querētes dein
de anxij parētes gnatū paruulū. postridie eū in fluuio inuenerūt. q̄ illico vꝛbis ꝑtoꝛi scelus demūciarūt. Is
ꝑtoꝛ iobānes de salis nobilis bꝛixtensiū ciuis legū doctoꝛ viso puero exboꝛruit facinⁱ⁹ ꝫ ꝓfestim vꝛbis iu
deos ꝓpbendit ꝫ eculeo eos sigillatim imponēs toꝛmētis astricti eo oꝛdine crimē retulerūt. q̄ diligēti ex
aminatione cognito iudeos ꝓdignis supplicijs exterminauit. Pꝛesul eo tpe vꝛbis Jo. binderbacb colle
git exāctū coꝛpꝰ ꝫ sepulcbꝛo mādat. multis euestigio cepit floꝛere miracul. Inde ex oī xꝑiano oꝛbe ppꝉoꝛ
ꝯcursus ad scti buius paruulī sepulcbꝛū est factus vt etiā vꝛbs iꝑa cū miraculis ꝫ opibus multis sit aucta
Coꝛpoꝛi vo iꝑius pueri tridentini ciues basilicam pulcbꝛam erexere

Part of a manuscript detailing an accusation that Jews ritually tortured a boy to death

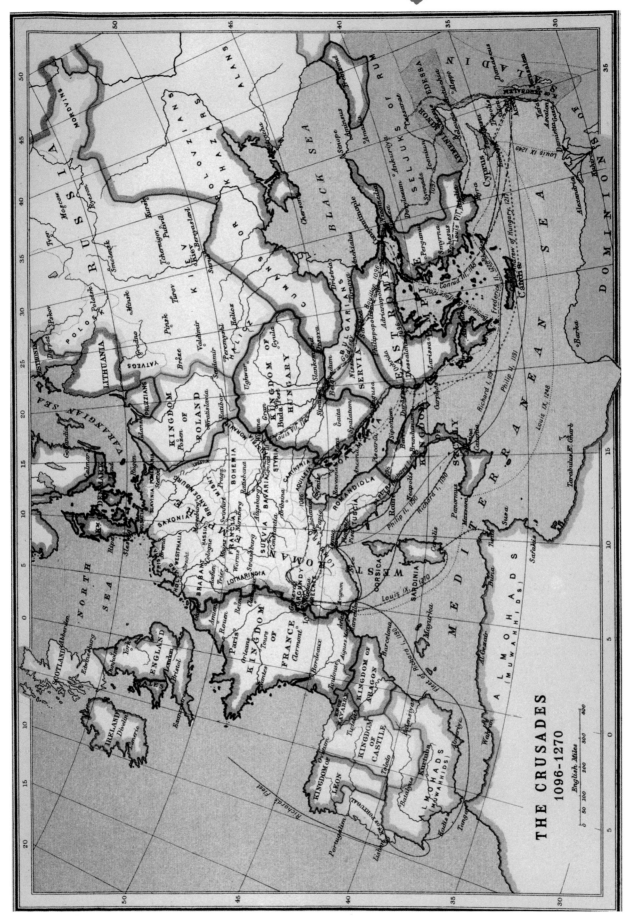

Map of the routes of the Crusaders from 1096–1270

THE CRUSADES
1096–1270

English Miles

'Crusaders embark for the Holy Land'

'The fleet of the Eighth Crusade in 1270'

'The defeat near Krak in 1163 of Nureddin by Geoffrey Martel of Anjou and Hugh of Lusignan'

'A clash between Saracens and Crusaders'

'Poverty wrestles with fortune'

'The Wheel of Fortune'

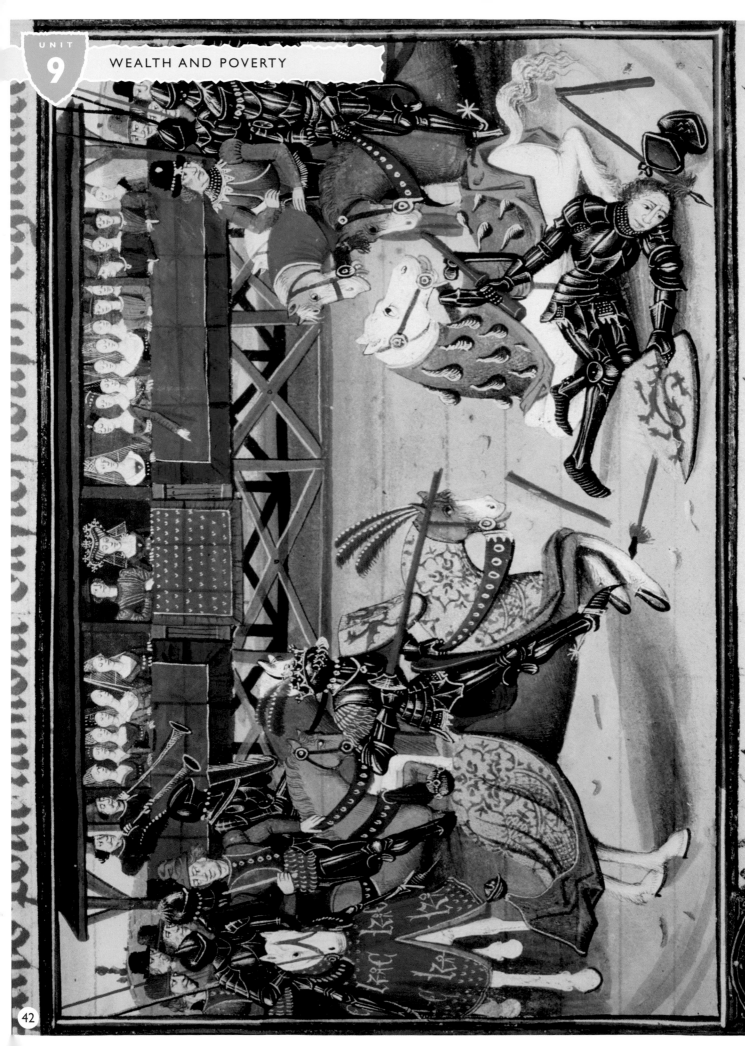

A tournament of 1179

'Lords and ladies in a garden'

'Richard II dining with the Dukes of York, Gloucester and Ireland'

43

A famine scene from 1470–80

A medieval family settle together by their fire

Masons at work watched by the nobility

Workmen and labourers and the tools of their trade

'The radical preacher John Ball (or Jean Balle) and ringleader Wat Tyler (or Waultre le Tieulier) during the Peasants' Revolt'

47

'Wat Tyler is killed'